J.E BAMIDE

ENCOURAGEMENT
SMALL IN DOSES

Encouragement In Small Doses

Copyright © 2015 by **J.E Bamidele Sturdivant**

Paperback ISBN 978-0-9960261-5-4
eBook ISBN 978-0-9960261-8-5
Library of Congress Control Number 2015956296

Published by
Godkulture Publishing
Chicago, Illinois

Phone: 773-696-0008
Email: publishing@godkulture.org
www.godkulturepublishing.com

Printed in the United States of America

Contents

Introduction

It is not everything that comes into mind that we are expected to express because there is a time for everything. The success of every man is based on *how* he speaks, *what* he says and *how* he says what he is saying. Many reputations have been damaged and characters assassinated due to someone speaking from a posture of emotional instability. If we took seriously the gravity of our words, we would be more cautious when we spoke.

If you want your life to be a source of encouragement to others, say only those things that will add value to the lives of others. We are admonished in Ephesians 4:29;

"Let no corrupt word proceed out of your mouth, but what is good for necessary edification, that it may impart grace to the hearers."

As this is done, you will find that you have the opportunity to be a blessing to others through your speech, thereby increasing your *sphere of encouragement and influence.*

As you build up and encourage others, you are bound to grow. As you read good content, you will grow intellectually. As you share what you have learned, to the benefit of others, you will grow as a friend and a person of influence. You will inspire them and they will be likely to encourage you, as well as others. Hence, your life becomes an instrument and conduit of healing to multitudes.

"A generous person will prosper; whoever refreshes others will be refreshed." (Proverbs 11:25)

This book, *Encouragement In Small Doses*, is a compilation of brief thoughts, instructive sayings and proverbs, divided into five categories, namely: *"Love Yourself"*, *"Relationships"*, *"Choosing to Change"*, *"Letting Go"* and *"Stay On Course."* They are woven together with relevant Scriptures to guide you on the right path, provide wisdom in decision making and offer daily inspiration. Pondering on them and sharing such, will chart a new course for a positive future for you, as well as others.

J.E Bamidele Sturdivant
District Heights
Maryland

Part One

Love Yourself

1

We are created "relational" beings, but a lack of love for 'self' can cause one to feel 'alone' even if they are in a crowd.

...You shall love your neighbor as yourself.
(Matthew 22:39)

2

Until one gets control of their *thought life*, they have no control over *their life*!

For as he thinks in his heart, so is he...
(Proverbs 23:7)

3

One's *life* is the sum total of experiences, choices and events. The common *thread* in each is *"you."* There is no one to blame!

... work out your own salvation with fear and trembling.
(Philippians 2:12)

4

The love of God accepts you *unconditionally*,
but it is not a license to live *recklessly*!

What shall we say then? Shall we continue in sin that grace may abound? Certainly not! How shall we who died to sin live any longer in it?
(Romans 6:1,2)

5

The same God, who was once your Savior, will one day be your Judge. Which *excuse* do you think He'll accept?

For we must all appear before the judgment seat of Christ, that each one may receive the things done in the body, according to what he has done, whether good or bad.
(II Corinthians 5:10)

6

Since nothing *catches* God by *surprise*, if you walk closely with Him, you won't be *caught off guard*, by the events of life!

For the eyes of the Lord run to and fro throughout the whole earth, to show Himself strong on behalf of those whose heart is loyal to Him...
(II Chronicles 16:9)

7 ∾

If "the joy of the Lord is your strength," do all that
you can to make Him happy.
Without faith, it's impossible.

*I love those who love me, and those who seek me diligently
will find me.*
(Proverbs 8:17)

8 ∾

Instead of asking God to "anoint" who or what you
want, get in His *will* and what you get will already be
anointed!

*Delight yourself also in the Lord, and He shall give you
the desires of your heart.*
(Psalm 37:4)

9

The God who "orders your *steps*" is also the One who "orders your *stops*!" Where has He told you not to go?

The steps of a good man are ordered by the Lord, and He delights in his way.
(Psalm 37:23)

10

Wanting what God has for you is not the issue;
Living the faith life to get it is!

But without faith it is impossible to please Him, for he who comes to God must believe that He is, and that He is a rewarder of those who diligently seek Him.
(Hebrews 11:6)

11

Peace with God and oneself, keeps you from becoming *perturbed* with the antics, actions and activities of people.

...but in everything by prayer and supplication, with thanksgiving, let your requests be made known to God; and the **peace** *of God, which surpasses all understanding, will guard your hearts and minds through Christ Jesus.*

(Philippians 4:6,7)

12

You are responsible for your *happiness*, but God is the giver of *joy*! Stop blaming other's for your *misery*!

Examine yourselves as to whether you are in the faith. Test yourselves. Do you not know yourselves, that Jesus Christ is in you?—unless indeed you are disqualified.

(II Corinthians 13:5)

13

In all that you are striving to "get," make getting
into His presence your priority!

*One thing I have desired of the Lord, that will I seek: that
I may dwell in the house of the Lord all the days of my life,
to behold the beauty of the Lord,
And to inquire in His temple.*

(Psalm 27:4)

14

Seek to live up to God's *desire for* you,
and not people's *expectation of* you!

*Many seek the ruler's favor, but justice for man comes
from the Lord.*

(Proverbs 29:26)

15

'IT' starts as a *thought*, turns into a *feeling*, moves to
an *act*, defines one's *character*, then is excused as one's
identity!

*A good man out of the good treasure of his heart brings
forth good things, and an evil man out of the evil treasure
brings forth evil things.*
(Matthew 12:35)

16

"Think about what you think about."
An *undisciplined thought-life* is the birth place
for an *out of control life*!

*Keep your heart with all diligence, for out of it spring the
issues of life.*
(Proverbs 4:23)

17 ⁓

Stop looking for something that makes you *feel* better and *start* looking for what *fills* you better.

And do not be drunk with wine, in which is dissipation; but be filled with the Spirit.
(Ephesians 5:18)

18 ⁓

The believability of your word is not based on the *sincerity* of the promise, but rather, on the *strength* of your character!

… Let your 'Yes' be 'Yes,' and your 'No,' 'No.' For whatever is more than these is from the evil one.
(Matthew 5:37)

19

The *mastering* of one's self keeps one from *becoming* a slave to anything else!

For when you were slaves of sin, you were free in regard to righteousness.
(Romans 6:20)

20

Your emotions are governed by your thoughts, and your thoughts are governed by information. Healthier information equals a better attitude!

How can a young man cleanse his way? By taking heed according to Your word. With my whole heart I have sought You...
(Psalm 119:9,10)

21 ✍

Until you are able to be *happy* with yourself,
you will never be *satisfied* being with anyone else!

I will praise You, for I am fearfully and wonderfully made;
Marvelous are Your works, and that my soul
knows very well.
(Psalm 139:14)

22 ✍

Having peace *with* God, the peace *of* God and peace
from God, makes it easy to be *at* peace with oneself
and with others!

When a man's ways please the Lord,
He makes even his enemies to be at peace with him.
(Proverbs 16:7)

23 ⌇

All movement is not progress! How much of your activity is actually advantageous?

Jesus answered and said to her, "Martha, Martha, you are worried and troubled about many things. But one thing is needed, and Mary has chosen that good part, which will not be taken away from her."
(Luke 10:41,42)

24 ⌇

In the midst of adversity, your *deliverance* is not in the multitude of voices, but in the *power* of a Word!

Your ears shall hear a word behind you, saying, "this is the way, walk in it," whenever you turn to the right hand or whenever you turn to the left.
(Isaiah 30:21)

25 ✍

To lead others out of 'darkness' you must either *have* light, *know* light or *be* light.
If none of these apply...*You* may be the one in the dark!

Let your light so shine before men, that they may see your good works and glorify your Father in heaven.
(Matthew 5:16)

26 ✍

Don't spend another day *lamenting* about your condition, if you're not willing to put in the *labor* to change it!

...that you also aspire to lead a quiet life, to mind your own business, and to work with your own hands, as we commanded you, that you may walk properly toward those who are outside, and that you may lack nothing.
(I Thessalonians 4:11,12)

27 ∽

The difference between the *pain* of your *past* and the *prospect* of your *future*, are the *choices* you make *today*!

I call heaven and earth as witnesses today against you, that I have set before you life and death, blessing and cursing; therefore choose life, that both you and your descendants may live.

(Deuteronomy 30:19)

28 ∽

What you *say* will determine what you *see*. You are either creating or cremating your world by your words!

For assuredly, I say to you, whoever says to this mountain, 'Be removed and be cast into the sea,' and does not doubt in his heart, but believes that those things he says will be done, he will have whatever he says. **(Mark 11:23)**

29

Experience may be the 'best teacher,' but the experience does *not* have to be yours for you to learn from it!

Now all these things happened to them as examples, and they were written for our admonition, upon whom the ends of the ages have come.
(I Corinthians 10:11)

30

If *experience* is a good *teacher*, then *pain* must be a *professor*.

Before I was afflicted I went astray, but now I keep Your word.
(Psalm 119:67)

31 ⌗

Why are you surprised that you have *nothing*, and are going *nowhere*, when you have done *nothing* to accomplish *anything*?!

A little sleep, a little slumber, a little folding of the hands to rest; so shall your poverty come like a prowler, and your need like an armed man.
(Proverbs 24:33,34)

32 ⌗

A "thing" (relationship, employment, 'blessing,' etc.), cannot be *of* God if it 'pulls' your commitment *from* God!.

But seek first the kingdom of God and His righteousness, and all these things shall be added to you.
(Matthew 6:33)

33

What is the hold up that you have not gotten the *big break*? You have not shown that you can be trusted on the *small scale*!

He who is faithful in what is least is faithful also in much; and he who is unjust in what is least is unjust also in much.
(Luke 16:10)

34

One's opinion *of* you is not God's conclusion *on* you! "I am" who God says "I am!"

For I know the thoughts that I think toward you, says the Lord, thoughts of peace and not of evil, to give you a future and a hope.
(Jeremiah 29:11)

35 ⟡

Time, breath and opportunity are three (3) components that you cannot get back once they are gone. Therefore, don't waste them!

See then that you walk circumspectly, not as fools but as wise, redeeming the time, because the days are evil.
(Ephesians 5:15,16)

36 ⟡

Your time and your breath are two (2) things that you cannot get back. Therefore, don't *waste* your breath on people who are not *worth* your time.

Blessed is the man who walks not in the counsel of the ungodly, nor stands in the path of sinners, nor sits in the seat of the scornful.
(Psalm 1:1)

37 ⌒

If you have to *undermine others* in an effort to *promote yourself*, there's a good chance God is *not backing you*!

For exaltation comes neither from the east nor from the west nor from the south. But God is the Judge: He puts down one, and exalts another.
(Psalm 75:6,7)

38 ⌒

Until God, for you, is *The Source* and not merely *a re-source*, you will see your blessing being *outsourced* to someone other than you!

Cursed is the man who trusts in man and makes flesh his strength, whose heart departs from the Lord.
(Jeremiah 17:5)

39

Occasionally, when God wants to *enlarge* your vision, He permits a *problem* that compels you to move *closer* to Him.

It is good for me that I have been afflicted, that I may learn Your statutes.
(Psalm 119:71)

40

Stop envying the existence of others.
Most of them are not happy with their own lives!

For those who live according to the flesh set their minds on the things of the flesh, but those who live according to the Spirit, the things of the Spirit.
(Romans 8:5)

41 ✐

A momentary lapse in judgment can abort all that
you've been believing for.
Ask yourself, "Is this worth all that?"

*Jesus said: No one, having put his hand to the plow,
and looking back, is fit for the kingdom of God.*
(Luke 9:62)

42 ✐

The *realm* of possibility is much more vast than
the *reality* of your problems! Where do you
choose to live?

*If you can believe, all things are possible
to him who believes.*
(Mark 9:23)

Part Two

Relationships

43 ∽

We all *need God* (dependent on), but we do not all *passionately want* (desperate for) Him. Re-examine the purity of your relationship!

As the deer pants for the water brooks, so pants my soul for You, O God. My soul thirsts for God, for the living God. When shall I come and appear before God?
(Psalm 42:1,2)

44 ∽

Try being in love with "you" before you *expect* someone else to!
You *attract* who you are, not what you want.

...You shall love your neighbor as yourself.
(Mark 12:31)

45

A daily passion to *please* God, will ultimately cause you to *disappoint* some people.

For am I now seeking the approval of man, or of God?
Or am I trying to please man?
If I were still trying to please man, I would not be a
servant of Christ.
(Galatians 1:10, ESV)

46

The need to be *wanted* by people, has kept many from being *accepted* by God! Be at "peace" with yourself.

Now acquaint yourself with Him, and be at peace;
thereby good will come to you. Receive, please, instruction
from His mouth, and lay up His words in your heart.
(Job 22:21,22)

47 ∽

Look closer...If you are sidetracked, backslidden or off-course, the culprit is not an *event*, but an *individual*.

You ran well. Who hindered you from obeying the truth? This persuasion does not come from Him who calls you. A little leaven leavens the whole lump.
(Galatians 5:7-9)

48 ∽

If you can't stand being by *yourself*,
why should someone want to be *alone* with you?

… but you shall love your neighbor as yourself …
(Leviticus 19:18)

49

What many think *others* should do for them,
they have yet to do for *themselves*.

*But let each one examine his own work, and then he will
have rejoicing in himself alone, and not in another. For
each one shall bear his own load.*
(Galatians 6:4,5)

50

The *person* God is asking you to let go, that you
"claim" you can't live without, at one time was a *total
stranger.*

*But Lot's wife looked back behind him, and she became a
pillar of salt.*
(Genesis 19:26)

51 ✌

Stay authentically you. Those who truly *want* you, *will change* their taste to accommodate your flavor.

Greater love has no one than this, than to lay down one's life for his friends.
(John 15:13)

52 ✌

If someone *loves* the God in you, they won't ask you to *compromise* your love for God! Is it flesh or spirit?

I say then: Walk in the Spirit, and you shall not fulfill the lust of the flesh. For the flesh lusts against the Spirit, and the Spirit against the flesh; and these are contrary to one another, so that you do not do the things that you wish.
(Galatians 5:16,17)

53

Demand emotional integrity! Does the individual love you for *who* you *are*, or merely for *what* you *do*?

A friend loves at all times, and a brother is born for adversity.
(Proverbs 17:17)

54

Do you *do for others* because you truly care, or does it *fill a need* in you?

Let each of you look out not only for his own interests, but also for the interests of others.
(Philippians 2:4)

55

You are not merely what you *see* in the *mirror*,
but what is *seen* in your *associations*.

Do not be deceived: "Evil company corrupts good habits."
(I Corinthians 15:33)

56

The longer you *stay* in relationships that God has
instructed you to get out of, the worse things will get.
Starve those relationships. Now!

*Do not enter the path of the wicked, and do not walk in
the way of evil. Avoid it, do not travel on it; turn away
from it and pass on.*
(Proverbs 4:14,15)

57

Those who have *no idea* what they are doing with *their life*, are quick to tell you how to *live yours*!

The righteous should choose his friends carefully, for the way of the wicked leads them astray.
(Proverbs 12:26)

58

If you forget who helped you get *where you are*, you'll go back to being *where you were* before they found you!

Whoever rewards evil for good, evil will not depart from his house.
(Proverbs 17:13)

59

If you don't have a *plan* for *where* you want *to be*,
it's easy to settle *with*, or *for* someone who is going
nowhere.

*Do not be unequally yoked together with unbelievers. For
what fellowship has righteousness with lawlessness? And
what communion has light with darkness?*
(II Corinthians 6:14)

60

If someone is stronger in their *weakness* than you are
in your *strength*, they will *drag* you down, before you
raise them up.

*… Shouldest thou help the ungodly, and love them that
hate the Lord? Therefore is wrath upon thee from before
the Lord.*
(II Chronicles 19:2, KJV)

61 ♒

Anyone *in* your life, not adding *to* your life,
(by virtue of their presence) is deducting *from*
your life!

As iron sharpens iron, so a man sharpens the countenance
of his friend.
(Proverbs 27:17)

62 ♒

Your greatness is not found in how many wise
people 'talk' with you, but in how many you
'listen' to!

Listen to counsel and receive instruction, that you may be
wise in your latter days.
(Proverbs 19:20)

63

Relational *disappointment* is the emotion felt from unrealistic *expectations* projected on someone whose *character* you failed to research!

All the ways of a man are pure in his own eyes, but the Lord weighs the spirits.
(Proverbs 16:2)

64

You really don't need *a lot of people* in your life; you simply need the *right person* for what *this* assignment requires!

A man of many companions may come to ruin, but there is a friend who sticks closer than a brother.
(Proverbs 18:24, ESV)

65

Some people are like "ticks," they *suck* the life out of you, then *fall off* and find someone else to *drain*.

…withdraw from every brother who walks disorderly…
For you yourselves know how you ought to follow us, for we
were not disorderly among you.
(II Thessalonians 3:6,7)

66

Don't fear the *enemy* that *attacks* you, but the fake *friend* that *hugs* you.

Faithful are the wounds of a friend,
but the kisses of an enemy are deceitful.
(Proverbs 27:6)

67 ∽

The mate who never does anything right and gets on your 'last' nerve, at one time, you couldn't live without! What does that say about you?

With all lowliness and gentleness, with longsuffering, bearing with one another in love, endeavoring to keep the unity of the Spirit in the bond of peace.
(Ephesians 4:2,3)

68 ∽

For the *one person* that 'you' are trying to win, there are *100* that God has sent your way that you ignored.

Those who are wise shall shine like the brightness of the firmament, and those who turn many to righteousness like the stars forever and ever.
(Daniel 12:3)

69

Everyone that *crosses your path* is not for *your* life. Some are sent for you to point *their* life *to the cross*.

...that God was in Christ reconciling the world to Himself, not imputing their trespasses to them, and has committed to us the word of reconciliation.
(II Corinthians 5:18,19)

70

The *wonder* of this journey called "Christianity" is this, God uses our *pain* to be someone else's *panacea*.

Let nothing be done through selfish ambition or conceit, but in lowliness of mind let each esteems others better than himself. Let each of you look out not only for his own interests, but also for the interests of others.
(Philippians 2:3,4)

71 ✑

Feeling a *connection to* someone, does not mean you
are to be in *relationship with* them!

*Let no one say when he is tempted, "I am tempted by
God;" for God cannot be tempted by evil, nor does He
Himself tempt anyone. But each one is tempted when he is
drawn away by his own desires and enticed.*
(James 1:13,14)

72 ✑

You cannot change what *people do*, but you *can*
change how *you react* so that what they do does
not affect or infect you.

*Let your speech always be with grace, seasoned with salt,
that you may know how you ought to answer each one.*
(Colossians 4:6)

73

A *sense of awareness* of your own presence, keeps you from being *intimidated* by the presence of others.

But sanctify the Lord God in your hearts, and always be ready to give a defense to everyone who asks you a reason for the hope that is in you, with meekness and fear.
(I Peter 3:15)

74

Some are so busy trying to be everyone's *answer*, until their own life has become a *question*.

I must work the works of Him who sent Me while it is day; the night is coming when no one can work.
(John 9:4)

75

If someone is *attracted* to the God in you,
then they'll *value* the 'house' where He lives.

*Do you not know that your body is the temple of the Holy
Spirit who is in you, whom you have from God, and you
are not your own?*
(I Corinthians 6:19)

76

Beware! When your *heart* continues to *long* for
someone who only *lusted* for your *body*.

*...that each of you should know how to possess his own
vessel in sanctification and honor.*
(I Thessalonians 4:3,4)

77 &

Those who are trying to *compete* with you, will never help to *complete* you! Aide or Adversary?

Then she said to him [Delilah said to Samson], "How can you say, 'I love you,' when your heart is not with me? You have mocked me these three times, and have not told me where your great strength lies."
(Judges 16:15)

78 &

It is harmful to give your *whole self* to someone who only saw you as a "*piece*."

Cursed is the man who trusts in man and makes flesh his strength, whose heart departs from the Lord.
(Jeremiah 17:5)

79

Stop trying to "make and force" those relationships to work. If God is closing that door, stop trying to pry it open. There's no profit.

I will instruct you and teach you in the way you should go; I will guide you with My eye. Do not be like the horse or like the mule, which have no understanding, which must be harnessed with bit and bridle.

(Psalm 32:8,9)

80

Loneliness has a way of causing one to get amnesia in relationship choices.
However, pain is a quick reminder!

Can a man take fire to his bosom, and his clothes not be burned? Can one walk on hot coals, and his feet not be seared?

(Proverbs 6:27,28)

81 ∽

It's ironic how we ignore those who *want* us, want those who *ignore* us, love those who *hurt* us, and hurt those who *love* us.

I, the Lord, search the heart, I test the mind, even to give every man according to his ways, according to the fruit of his doings.
(Jeremiah 17:10)

82 ∽

In each person's life there is a John and a Judas. One shows 'affection,' the other shows 'love.' All friends are *not created* equal!

Even my own familiar friend in whom I trusted, who ate my bread, Has lifted up his heel against me.
(Psalm 41:9)

Part Three

*Choosing
to
Change*

83

The "changing of the *calendar*" does not guarantee
the "changing of one's *character*."
Happy New You!

*So teach us to number our days, that we may gain
a heart of wisdom.*
(Psalm 90:12)

84

Only say what you want *to see*. Your *words* create
your *world*.

*…As I live,' says the Lord, 'just as you have spoken in
My hearing, so I will do to you.*
(Numbers 14:28)

85

Instead of *lamenting* about the past bad decisions, why not *learn* from them and make the next one better!

For a righteous man may fall seven times and rise again…
(Proverbs 24:16)

86

Pretending you're *flawless* does *not* make you *perfect*.
Admitting your flaws shows
you are "being" *perfected*!

If we say that we have no sin, we deceive ourselves, and the truth is not in us. If we confess our sins, He is faithful and just to forgive us our sins and to cleanse us from all unrighteousness.
(I John 1:8,9)

87 ⚜

God is a God of *standards*. If you claim to be His, why do you settle for just *anything*?

Therefore you shall be perfect, just as your Father in heaven is perfect.
(Matthew 5:48)

88 ⚜

Many refuse to *develop* the *character* that is necessary to *sustain* them in a crisis. Hence, they collapse each time one arises!

...giving all diligence, add to your faith virtue, to virtue knowledge, to knowledge self-control, to self-control perseverance, to perseverance godliness, to godliness brotherly kindness, and to brotherly kindness love.

(II Peter 1:5-7)

89

One gains victory over *sin* when the desire to please the *Savior* is greater than the desire to please *self*.

For to be carnally minded is death, but to be spiritually minded is life and peace. Because the carnal mind is enmity against God;...So then, those who are in the flesh cannot please God.

(Romans 8:6-8)

90

One does not sin because he doesn't *hate sin* enough. He sins because he doesn't *love God* enough!

No one can serve two masters; for either he will hate the one and love the other, or else he will be loyal to the one and despise the other. You cannot serve God and mammon.

(Matthew 6:24)

91 ∽

Disobedience or partial obedience may cause us
to miss what God promised or not receive what
we prayed for.

If I regard iniquity in my heart, the Lord not hear.
(Psalm 66:18)

92 ∽

Just because God does not *kill you instantly*, does
not mean that you have *life eternally*!

*Because the sentence against an evil work is not executed
speedily, therefore the heart of the sons of men is fully set
in them to do evil.*
(Ecclesiastes 8:11)

93 ❧

An *abundance of heavenly favor* cannot make up for a
lack of *personal integrity*.

*Better is the poor who walks in his integrity than
one perverse in his ways, though he be rich.*
(Proverbs 28:6)

94 ❧

Never mistake someone *being* anointed for
having integrity!

*Many will say to me in that day, Lord, Lord, have we not
prophesied in thy name? And in thy name have cast out devils?
And in thy name done many wonderful works? And then will
I profess unto them, I never knew you: depart from me, ye that
work iniquity.*
(Matthew 7:22,23, KJV)

95 ∽

What many are constantly *praying* for, would automatically be released if they would simply *live holy*!

Behold, the Lord's hand is not shortened, that it cannot save; nor His ear heavy, that it cannot hear. But your iniquities have separated you from your God; and your sins have hidden His face from you, so that He will not hear.

(Isaiah 59:1,2)

96 ∽

Much of what many are "begging" God for is *freely given* when their *lifestyle* is in alignment with His Word!

If you abide in Me, and My words abide in you, you will ask what you desire, and it shall be done for you. By this My Father is glorified, that you bear much fruit; so you will be My disciples.

(John 15:7,8)

97 &

Make *mistakes*, probably. That's a part of the
learning process. Make the *same* mistakes, never.
That's a *sign* one hasn't *learned*.

*When I was a child, I spoke as a child, I understood as a
child, I thought as a child;
but when I became a man, I put away childish things.*
(I Corinthians 13:11)

98 &

Do *now* what you are going to *wish* you had done
later. Procrastination is not your friend.

*He who observes the wind will not sow, and he who regards
the clouds will not reap.*
(Ecclesiastes 11:4)

99

If we *understood* the true power of our words, we would *talk* and *text* less non-sense!

Let your moderation be known unto all men.
The Lord is at hand.
(Philippians 4:5, KJV)

100

Reputations can be *damaged* by a tweet, status update or text.
Emotional stability is a must in the cyber world.

The Lord God has given me the tongue of the learned, that I should know how to speak a word in season to him who is weary. He awakens me morning by morning, He awakens my ear to hear as the learned.

(Isaiah 50:4)

101 ✑

Like David, we can *handle* the Goliaths in our lives
when we *see* them coming.
In view of this, Solomon said *catch* the "little
foxes," they *cause* giant failure!

*Catch us the foxes, the little foxes that spoil the vines,
for our vines have tender grapes.*
(Song of Solomon 2:15)

102 ✑

Once you have made a *spiritual decision* to
live *holy*, send your *mind, emotions* and *body* a memo!

*…present your bodies a living sacrifice, holy, acceptable to God,
which is your reasonable service.
And do not be conformed to this world, but be transformed
by the renewing of your mind, that you may prove what is that
good and acceptable and perfect will of God.*

(Romans 12:1,2)

103 ✑

Many are so active in the *busy-ness* of life,
until they are *overlooking* the subtle *move* of God!

For since the beginning of the world Men have not heard
nor perceived by the ear,
nor has the eye seen any God besides You, who acts for the
one who waits for Him.
(Isaiah 64:4)

104 ✑

In the face of *overwhelming odds*, God is "waiting
on you," to *wait on Him*!

Those who wait on the Lord shall renew their strength;
they shall mount up with wings like eagles, they shall run
and not be weary, they shall walk and not faint.
(Isaiah 40:31)

105 ⟋∽

If you have difficulty *hearing*, *knowing* and *discerning*
God's voice, it could be that you are *living* a lie.

My sheep hear My voice, and I know them,
and they follow Me.
(John 10:27)

106 ⟋∽

Saying, "I know I need to change" does *not* mean
that you actually *intend* to change! *Do* more than
talk.

In all labor there is profit, but idle chatter leads only to
poverty.
(Proverbs 14:23)

107 &

Elevation is not given to the "most gifted."
It is 'graced' to the one who stays *humble*!

Humble yourselves in the sight of the Lord,
and He will lift you up.
(James 4:10)

108 &

Your *title* does not *entitle* you to ever "graduate"
from the position of *servant*!

His lord said to him, 'Well done, good and faithful
servant; you were faithful over a few things,
I will make you ruler over many things.
Enter into the joy of your lord.'
(Matthew 25:21)

109 ✌

Many *claim* that they desire to *excel* and be *promoted*, yet they *complain* when *God* requires them to "live" *above average.*

I pray, that your love may abound still more and more in knowledge and all discernment, that you may approve the things that are excellent, that you may be sincere and without offense till the day of Christ.
(Philippians 1:9,10)

110 ✌

The *high things* that God *promises* are not released to those whose "lifestyles" are *low down*!

If then you were raised with Christ, seek those things which are above, where Christ is, sitting at the right hand of God. Set your mind on things above, not on things on the earth.
(Colossians 3:1,2)

111

When God puts *pressure* on you, it is *not* for "discomfort," but because a *breakthrough* is about to "come forth."

A woman, when she is in labor, has sorrow because her hour has come; but as soon as she has given birth to the child, she no longer remembers the anguish, for joy that a human being has been born into the world.

(John 16:21)

112

There *is* a "place" where what once was *impossible* can be your *normal.* Strive to stay *in Him*!

He who dwells in the secret place of the Most High shall abide under the shadow of the Almighty.
I will say of the Lord, "He is my refuge and my fortress; My God, in Him I will trust."

(Psalm 91:1,2)

113 ᕲᕲ

You can't say, "I'm just doing me," then *blame* everyone else for how *your life* turns out. It takes 'grace' to listen!

They would have none of my counsel and despised my every rebuke. Therefore they shall eat the fruit of their own way, and be filled to the full with their own fancies.
(Proverbs 1:30,31)

114 ᕲᕲ

Most don't realize what they *should have* learned until they are *required* to *do* what they *don't know*!

The hand of the diligent will rule, but the lazy man will be put to forced labor.
(Proverbs 12:24)

115

Tell the *truth*, even if by doing so, you *expose yourself* as having *told* a *lie*! Forgiveness is available!

The truthful lip shall be established forever, but a lying tongue is but for a moment.
(Proverbs 12:19)

116

The *miraculous* is available to those who *choose* to live *beyond* the *mundane*!

Eye has not seen, nor ear heard, nor have entered into the heart of man the things which God has prepared for those who love Him.
(I Corinthians 2:9)

117 ∽

If you *return* to *intimacy* with God,
resisting the *temptation* to sin comes naturally!

Therefore submit to God. Resist the devil and he will flee
from you. Draw near to God and He will draw near to
you. Cleanse your hands, you sinners; and purify your
hearts, you double-minded.
(James 4:7,8)

118 ∽

God's *promise to* you, can only be *aborted by* you!
Stay *in faith* and *out of* doubt.

And not being weak in faith, he did not consider his own body,
already dead...and the deadness of Sarah's womb. He did not waver
at the promise of God through unbelief, but was strengthened in
faith, giving glory to God, and being fully convinced that what He
had promised He was also able to perform.
(Romans 4:19-21)

119 ✎

How you "feel" about *people*, is a 'measuring rod'
of how much you *love you*.

*You shall not take vengeance, nor bear any grudge against
the children of your people, but you shall love your
neighbor as yourself: I am the Lord.*
(Leviticus 19:18)

120 ✎

Some of the people that others are *taking for
granted*, God is *taking for His glory*!

*Do not forget to entertain strangers, for by so doing some
have unwittingly entertained angels.*
(Hebrews 13:2)

121

Many *don't witness* because they have become
'numb' to the *reality of hell*...
nor have they thought of their
family members there!

The fruit of the righteous is a tree of life,
and he who wins souls is wise.
(Proverbs 11:30)

122

Everyone that you meet is a *potential asset* to the
Kingdom. Don't you be a *deficit*
by failing to *witness*!

How beautiful upon the mountains are the feet of him
who brings good news, who proclaims peace, who brings glad
tidings of good things, who proclaims salvation, who says
to Zion, "Your God reigns!"
(Isaiah 52:7)

Part Four

Letting Go

123 ✤

God can only fill the areas that He has *access* to.
Secret, subtle sins are *pin numbers* that
"lock" Him out!

*Who can understand his errors? Cleanse me from secret faults.
Keep back Your servant also from presumptuous sins; let them
not have dominion over me. Then I shall be blameless, and I
shall be innocent of great transgression.*
(Psalm 19:12,13)

124 ✤

Unforgiveness keeps you *permanently* tied to the one
whom you claim causes you *pain*.
Forgiveness sets *you* free!

*Whenever you stand praying, if you have anything against
anyone, forgive him, that your Father in heaven may also forgive
you your trespasses. But if you do not forgive, neither will your
Father in heaven forgive your trespasses.*
(Mark 11:25,26)

125 ✎

Whenever *pride* makes you *think* that you are the *exception* to the rule, *reality* shows you that you are just another *statistic*!

Pride goes before destruction,
and a haughty spirit before a fall.
(Proverbs 16:18)

126 ✎

God can't send who will "fill" the *empty place* in your heart, as long as you 'keep' an *occupant* in your bed!

He who covers his sins will not prosper, but whoever confesses and forsakes them will have mercy.
(Proverbs 28:13)

127 ✒

Your *love for God* is measured in *direct proportion* to
your *hatred for sin*!
How is your love life?

*…How then can I do this great wickedness,
and sin against God?*
(Genesis 39:9)

128 ✒

Bitterness is the expiration date on forgiving!

*Let all bitterness, wrath, anger, clamor, and evil speaking
be put away from you, with all malice.*
(Ephesians 4:31)

129 ✍

People ask God to *do something new* in their lives, then complain when He starts *removing old relationships.*

No one sews a piece of unshrunk cloth on an old garment; or else the new piece pulls away from the old, and the tear is made worse. And no one puts new wine into old wineskins; or else the new wine bursts the wineskins, the wine is spilled, and the wineskins are ruined. But new wine must be put into new wineskins.

(Mark 2:21,22)

130 ✍

Your past is a *returned check* that tells you *what you spent*, but you cannot respend it. File it, use it as a point of reference and move on!

Let your eyes look straight ahead,
and your eyelids look right before you.
(Proverbs 4:25)

131 &

Until you can *talk* about the *situation* that hurt you, without feeling *bitterness* towards the individuals who did it, you're not free!

Be angry, and do not sin: do not let the sun go down on your wrath, nor give place to the devil.
(Ephesians 4:26,27)

132 &

Many *complain* when they don't get *credit* for what they do, as if they are *owed glory*, when all that they have, they *got by grace*!

For He says to Moses, "I will have mercy on whomever I will have mercy, and I will have compassion on whomever I will have compassion." So then it is not of him who wills, nor of him who runs, but of God who shows mercy.
(Romans 9:15,16)

133

What stagnates most people is *not* an "intimidating fact" about tomorrow (unknown), but rather an "emotional memory" from yesterday (known)!

...if anyone is in Christ, he is a new creation; old things have passed away; behold, all things have become new.
(II Corinthians 5:17)

134

Struggle is a "sign" that you are still *fighting*. However, some struggles, you shouldn't be still *having*!

... the Lord does not save with sword and spear; for the battle is the Lord's...
(I Samuel 17:47)

135

Every *unkindness* that you have experienced that you thought was 'unforgiveable,' in view of eternity...it's not that serious!

... "Lord, how often shall my brother sin against me, and I forgive him? Up to seven times?"
Jesus said to him, "I do not say to you, up to seven times, but up to seventy times seven.
(Matthew 18:21,22)

136

When you are *desperate* for your *future*, you must be *content* to leave some people in your *past*.

Look carefully then how you walk, not as unwise but as wise, making the best use of the time, because the days are evil. Therefore do not be foolish, but understand what the will of the Lord is.
(Ephesians 5:15-17, ESV)

137 ✒

Come up higher: your *elevation* may cause *elimination* of some you used to have a relationship with. All can't handle your altitude.

Therefore we also, since we are surrounded by so great a cloud of witnesses, let us lay aside every weight, and the sin which so easily ensnares us, and let us run with endurance the race that is set before us.

(Hebrews 12:1)

138 ✒

The *power* of God's *promise* and *presence* is what *propels* you *pass* the *pain* of your *past!*

Looking unto Jesus, the author and finisher of our faith, who for the joy that was set before Him endured the cross, despising the shame, and has sat down at the right hand of the throne of God.

(Hebrews 12:2)

139 ✒

Unforgiveness gives the person who offended you *power over* you. Forgive, not because they're right, but so *you can be set free*!

Be kind to one another, tenderhearted, forgiving one another, even as God in Christ forgave you.
(Ephesians 4:32)

140 ✒

The *greatest damage* of, whatever your *sin*, is that it keeps *those* who are "watching" *you* from "seeing" *Him*!

Take heed to yourself and to the doctrine. Continue in them, for in doing this you will save both yourself and those who hear you.
(I Timothy 4:16)

141 ✍

Once an individual has shown you who they really are, *adjust* the way *you move* instead of *trying* to *change* the way they are!

Go from the presence of a foolish man, when you do not perceive in him the lips of knowledge.
(Proverbs 14:7)

142 ✍

If someone tells you, "don't trust me, I've got issues, people say I'm crazy…"
Believe them and *leave them*! You are *not* the *Messiah*!

…For out of the abundance of the heart his mouth speaks.
(Luke 6:45)

143 ❧

The moment you see *Sovereignty* you see your *true self*. When you are in the Presence of the *Holy God*, He compels you to look at *you*!

Woe is me, for I am undone! Because I am a man of unclean lips, and I dwell in the midst of a people of unclean lips; For my eyes have seen the King, The Lord of hosts.
(Isaiah 6:5)

144 ❧

You can spend so much time *listening* to *self, calling* it *God*, until when it comes to *hearing* from God, all you've got is *self*!

Lay aside all filthiness and overflow of wickedness, and receive with meekness the implanted word, which is able to save your souls.
(James 1:21)

145 ❧

The *ability* of God is often "hindered" by our lack
of *availability* to Him.
More of Him means *less of you*!

He must increase, but I must decrease.
(John 3:30)

146 ❧

If you are *constantly* asking God, "how much
longer" and "why," most likely you are failing the
test of *faith*!

*My brethren, count it all joy when you fall into various
trials, knowing that the testing of your faith produces
patience. But let patience have its perfect work, that you
may be perfect and complete, lacking nothing.*
(James 1:2-4)

147 ∾

Time and *people* can pass, but until you release the
bitterness of an offense,
you remain a *prisoner* to the *event*.

*Pursue peace with all people, and holiness, without which no
one will see the Lord: looking carefully lest anyone fall short of
the grace of God; lest any root of bitterness springing up cause
trouble, and by this many become defiled.*
(Hebrews 12:14,15)

148 ∾

God does not care how much it may *cost*
or how far we have to go to *obey* His Word.

*He who does not take his cross and follow after Me is not
worthy of Me. He who finds his life will lose it, and he
who loses his life for My sake will find it.*
(Matthew 10:38,39)

149 ⚜

The *smarter* you try to 'appear' *going against* the will of God, the *dumber* the devil *makes* you *look*!

There is a way that seems right to a man,
but its end is the way of death.
(Proverbs 14:12)

150 ⚜

Father...I have resigned my *wants* to Your *will*, so that You can have Your *way* in my *world*!

... *"O My Father, if it is possible, let this cup pass from Me; nevertheless, not as I will, but as You will."*
(Matthew 26:39)

151

If you *really* want what you *say* you want, as badly as you *claim* to want it, letting go of what you *have* is easy!

Then He said to them all, "If anyone desires to come after Me, let him deny himself, and take up his cross daily, and follow Me."
(Luke 9:23)

152

Is what you're *compromising to keep*, worth what you *stand to lose?*

… Is it time to receive money and to receive clothing,…? Therefore the leprosy of Naaman shall cling to you and your descendants forever." And he went out from his presence leprous, as white as snow.
(II Kings 5:26,27)

153 ⌘

Until your *passion* for your *future* is greater than your *appetite* for the *present*, you will *eat* the *leftovers* of your *past!*

The night is far spent, the day is at hand. Therefore let us cast off the works of darkness, and let us put on the armor of light. Let us walk properly, as in the day, not in revelry and drunkenness, not in lewdness and lust, not in strife and envy.

(Romans 13:12,13)

154 ⌘

A "sacrifice" is *not* a *sacrifice* if you do not *feel* it when you let it go! What has God asked you to *release?*

If anyone comes to Me and does not hate his father and mother, wife and children, brothers and sisters, yes, and his own life also, he cannot be My disciple.

(Luke 14:26)

155 ∽

Coming into what *God* has *for you*, means leaving
people, mindsets and limitations that you have
accepted for yourself!

*Therefore, if anyone is in Christ, he is a new creation; old
things have passed away;
behold, all things have become new.*
(II Corinthians 5:17)

156 ∽

How many times must a person do the *same thing*
before you *realize* it's *not an event*, nor *a bad day*, but
who they are?

*A fool has no delight in understanding,
but in expressing his own heart.*
(Proverbs 18:2)

157 ✍

Don't allow *mediocre* individuals, with *limited* vision,
to draw you into *unproductive* conversations that
keep you *stagnant*.

*But avoid all empty (vain, useless, idle) talk, for it will
lead people into more and more ungodliness.*
(II Timothy 2:16, AMP)

158 ✍

If "all *hell* is *breaking loose*" in your life, get excited.
Why? A "house divided against itself can't stand."

*Yes, and all who desire to live godly in Christ Jesus
will suffer persecution.*
(II Timothy 3:12)

159 ✑

Jesus had the power to prevent the *agony* on the cross, but He was concerned about you. This *sacrificial love* requires that you have to let go of self so as to see as God sees.

I can of Myself do nothing. As I hear, I judge; and My judgment is righteous, because I do not seek My own will but the will of the Father who sent Me.

(John 5:30)

160 ✑

The *discomforts* that you are experiencing are the *labor pains* of a dream coming forth. Don't rebuke it, *give birth*!

For I consider that the sufferings of this present time are not worthy to be compared with the glory which shall be revealed in us.

(Romans 8:18)

161 ✐

Have a "bad moment?" Possibly. Have a "bad day?" Never! Don't allow a *temporary* misfortune to rob you of a *day* of *possibility*!

It is of the Lord's mercies that we are not consumed, because his compassions fail not. They are new every morning: great is thy faithfulness.
(Lamentations 3:22,23, KJV)

162 ✐

You can *get pass* anything that *anyone* has ever done to you in the *past*, once *you* decide to *move* from that place of pain!

Casting all your care upon Him, for He cares for you.
(I Peter 5:7)

Part Five

Stay On Course

163 ∽

You may be too young to *plan a family* right now, but you are not too young to begin setting up their spiritual inheritance. Hence, *seek God* with all your heart.

...Blessed is the man who fears the Lord, Who delights greatly in His commandments. His descendants will be mighty on earth; the generation of the upright will be blessed. Wealth and riches will be in his house, and his righteousness endures forever.
(Psalm 112:1-3)

164 ∽

The life of holiness is in levels, *you can begin* that journey to higher levels of holiness, by diligently *seeking God daily* in worship, meditation on His Word and also living by it.

Blessed are those who hunger and thirst for righteousness, for they shall be filled. Blessed are the pure in heart, For they shall see God.
(Matthew 5:6,8)

165 〰

While you are merely *expressing yourself*, someone
is *assessing your stand*! How does Jesus 'look' on
twitter, instagram and facebook?

You will know them by their fruits…
(Matthew 7:16)

166 〰

How many *souls* are in the *kingdom* because of
you? How many will go to *hell* because you did *not*
witness?

You are the light of the world. A city that is set on a hill
cannot be hidden. Nor do they light
a lamp and put it under a basket, but on a lampstand, and it
gives light to all who are in the house.

(Matthew 5:14,15)

167 &

Your productivity in life depends on how you allow Jesus (The Word) to pierce all your being, because it is only through Him that you can truly thrive in this world.

Then Jesus said to those Jews who believed Him, "If you abide in My Word, you are My disciples indeed. And you shall know the truth, and the truth shall make you free."

(John 8:31,32)

168 &

You must *hate* what God hates and *love* what He loves, *hold on* to what He says to hold on to, and *let go* of what and who He says to let go of.

Who may ascend into the hill of the Lord? Or who may stand in His holy place? He who has clean hands and a pure heart, who has not lifted up his soul to an idol, nor sworn deceitfully. He shall receive blessing from the Lord, and righteousness from the God of his salvation.

(Psalm 24:3-5)

169 ✍

What detours one in the course of their destiny, are the things that they *know* to do, but *don't* carry out. These are the things that usually make you fall.

But you must continue in the things which you have learned and been assured of, knowing from whom you have learned them.
(II Timothy 3:14)

170 ✍

The victory of *this* moment is *determined* by what you "stood for" *before* this moment *arrived*.

Now thanks be to God who always leads us in triumph in Christ, and through us diffuses the fragrance of His knowledge in every place.
(II Corinthians 2:14)

171 ✍

Just because you *struggled* to get *to* this level,
does *not* mean that you can "relax" now that you
are *here*!

Woe to you who are at ease in Zion…
(Amos 6:1)

172 ✍

What do you want most, His 'Presence' or His
'presents?' Chasing after the one may forfeit the other.
Choose wisely!

*Jesus answered them, "Most assuredly, I say to you, you seek Me,
not because you saw the signs, but because you ate of the loaves
and were filled. Do not labor for the food which perishes, but for
the food which endures to everlasting life, which the Son of Man
will give you, because God the Father has set His seal on Him."*
(John 6:26,27)

173 ✑

Until you *define* what your *life's mission* is,
you will *spend time* doing "stuff" but never *fulfill*
destiny!

Then I said, 'Behold, I have come - In the volume of the
book it is written of Me - To do Your will, O God.
(Hebrews 10:7)

174 ✑

Once you *purpose to be* a "problem solver,"
there will *never be* a shortage of assignments or
rewards available!

…Take heed to the ministry which you have received in
the Lord, that you may fulfill it.
(Colossians 4:17)

175 ℘

God's plan is not changing, but you have to *conform* to His standards to have an *enduring transformation* in your life.

But we all, with unveiled face, beholding as in a mirror the glory of the Lord, are being transformed into the same image from glory to glory, just as by the Spirit of the Lord.
(II Corinthians 3:18)

176 ℘

Everyone has at least one *talent*, if used during their *tenure* of *time*, can gain the *treasure* needed to handle their *troubles*!

As each one has received a gift, minister it to one another, as good stewards of the manifold grace of God.
(I Peter 4:10)

177 ✌

For whatever *assignment* God has given you,
there is a *place*, a *need* and an *anointing* for it!

A man's gift makes room for him,
and brings him before great men.
(Proverbs 18:16)

178 ✌

Once you are *comfortable* with *your place* in the
Kingdom, *other people's progress* will
cease to be *intimidating*!

Like a bird that wanders from its nest is a man who
wanders from his place.
(Proverbs 27:8)

179 ✍

If you live by the motto, "How much *sin* can I *commit* and *still* go to *heaven*?" You may be *off the path* to get there!

Whoever abides in Him does not sin. Whoever sins has neither seen Him nor known Him. Little children, let no one deceive you. He who practices righteousness is righteous, just as He is righteous. He who sins is of the devil, for the devil has sinned from the beginning... **(I John 3:6-8)**

180 ✍

You can *never* expect God to give you *His peace* in your life, when you continuously violate *His purpose* for your life!

Oh, that you had heeded My commandments! Then your peace would have been like a river, and your righteousness like the waves of the sea.
(Isaiah 48:18)

181 ✍

The greatness of a person lies in his ability to *find* something or someone else stronger than him to *lean* on.

The LORD is my rock and my fortress and my deliverer; my God, my strength, in whom I will trust; my shield and the horn of my salvation, my stronghold.
(Psalm 18:2)

182 ✍

Our ego has a way of disguising our true self, so it requires some effort to unveil it. However, to *be* yourself, and be at peace *with* yourself, you must truly *know* yourself.

But when he came to himself, he said, 'How many of my father's hired servants have bread enough and to spare, and I perish with hunger!'
(Luke 15:17)

183 ∽

Moral uprightness without mental and heart purity is not true sanctification. Instead, mental and heart sanctification will always produce moral uprightness.

Now may the God of peace Himself sanctify you completely; and may your whole spirit, soul, and body be preserved blameless at the coming of our Lord Jesus Christ.
(I Thessalonians 5:23)

184 ∽

Many make the gross mistake of filling their "personal agendas" at the expense of Heaven's candidates!

But the Lord said to Samuel, "Do not look at his appearance or at his physical stature, because I have refused him. For the Lord does not see as man sees; for man looks at the outward appearance, but the Lord looks at the heart.
(I Samuel 16:7)

185 ℘

God has *proven His love* for you through *His death*.
Have you *shown your love* for Him through *your life?*

*A new commandment I give to you, that you love one
another; as I have loved you, that you also love one
another. By this all will know that you are My disciples,
if you have love for one another.*
(John 13:34,35)

186 ℘

To stay focused on what *God has* for you, you can't
waste time *being envious* of what He's *doing for*
someone else!

*Brethren, I do not count myself to have apprehended; but one
thing I do, forgetting those things which are behind and reaching
forward to those things which are ahead, I press toward the
goal for the prize of the upward call of God in Christ Jesus.*
(Philippians 3:13,14)

187 ✑

One must know their *standards* before they are tempted to *compromise*. The *pressure* of the moment won't *allow* you to *choose*!

Nevertheless the solid foundation of God stands, having this seal: "The Lord knows those who are His," and, "Let everyone who names the name of Christ depart from iniquity."
(II Timothy 2:19)

188 ✑

Chasing after the trappings of success, trying to fill the emptiness inside, *cannot satisfy you* because you have a God shaped vacuum in you which *can only be filled by Him.*

Why do you spend money for what is not bread, and your wages for what does not satisfy? Listen carefully to Me, and eat what is good, and let your soul delight itself in abundance. Incline your ear, and come to Me. Hear, and your soul shall live; and I will make an everlasting covenant with you....
(Isaiah 55:2,3)

189 ∾

Many *stumble* from one career to the other, one relationship to another, and from one addiction to a different one; simply because they have *no direction* in life.

Your Word is a lamp to my feet and a light to my path.
(Psalm 119:105)

190 ∾

Just like a dog will *get back up* to follow his master, when it hears the proper commands, likewise you can *take your mind back* to the Word and tell it to stay put.

You will keep him in perfect peace, whose mind is stayed on You, because he trusts in You.
(Isaiah 26:3)

191 ✍

When *adversity* is *screaming*, and God is *silent*...
Be Still! He is *working* on things behind the *scene*
before He brings it on the '*seen*.'

*For My thoughts are not your thoughts, nor are your ways
My ways, says the Lord. For as the heavens are higher than
the earth, so are My ways higher than your ways, And My
thoughts than your thoughts.*

(Isaiah 55:8,9)

192 ✍

Faith "untried" is not faith at all. This current *trial*
is for you to "see" what you *think* you 'walk by!'

*My brethren, count it all joy when you fall into various
trials, knowing that the testing of your faith produces
patience. But let patience have its perfect work, that you
may be perfect and complete, lacking nothing.*

(James 1:2-4)

193 ✑

Real *faith demands* that you live above *'see'* level.
When it doesn't *make sense*, it then *takes faith*!

*By faith we understand that the worlds were framed by the
word of God, so that the things which are seen were not
made of things which are visible.*
(Hebrews 11:3)

194 ✑

Stop preaching and talking about *faith* if your main
concern is what's going to be on your tax-return.
Trust God and *move*!

*But someone will say, "You have faith, and I have
works." Show me your faith without your works, and I
will show you my faith by my works.*
(James 2:18)

195 ✧

When dealing with spiritual problems,
neither *flesh* nor *emotions* are useful *weapons*!

For though we walk in the flesh, we do not war according to the flesh. For the weapons of our warfare are not carnal but mighty in God for pulling down strongholds, casting down arguments and every high thing that exalts itself against the knowledge of God, bringing every thought into captivity to the obedience of Christ.

(II Corinthians 10:3-5)

196 ✧

You cannot wait until the *enemy attacks* to decide
to *put on* your *armor.*

Finally, my brethren, be strong in the Lord and in the power of His might.
Put on the whole armor of God, that you may be able to stand against the wiles of the devil.

(Ephesians 6:10,11)

197 ✍

Our uncertainty of where we stand *with* God
makes us unable to boldly stand *for* God.

*What then shall we say to these things? If God is for us,
who can be against us?*
(Romans 8:31)

198 ✍

Being an *answer* to the *problems* on earth, not only
make the world a better place, but also make your
presence irreplaceable!

*For the earnest expectation of the creation eagerly waits
for the revealing of the sons of God.*
(Romans 8:19)

199 ✑

Live in continual *expectation*, otherwise, how will you know when God has *answered* your *request?*

be thou in the fear of the Lord all the day long.
For surely there is an end; and thine expectation shall not
be cut off.
(Proverbs 23:17,18, KJV)

200 ✑

Many have made the *mistake* of pursuing *their passion* instead of fulfilling H*is purpose!*

There are many plans in a man's heart,
Nevertheless the Lord's counsel - that will stand.
(Proverbs 19:21)

201 ⌇

We often find the *place* where God was trying to *put* us, when we are *rejected* by people, in whose life we don't *fit*.

The stone which the builders rejected has become the chief cornerstone. This was the Lord's doing, and it is marvelous in our eyes.
(Matthew 21:42)

202 ⌇

The *journey* with the Lord is neither a *sprint* nor a *marathon*, but a *walk*.
Pace yourself...your *steps* are ordered!

...since we are surrounded by so great a cloud of witnesses, let us lay aside every weight, and the sin which so easily ensnares us, and let us run with endurance the race that is set before us.
(Hebrews 12:1)

203 ✌

Exposure is the ingredient that *expands*
one's *expectation*.

*Then He brought him [God brought Abram] outside and
said, "Look now toward heaven, and count the stars if
you are able to number them." And He said to him, "So
shall your descendants be."*
(Genesis 15:5)

204 ✌

To obtain the *impossible*, one must be willing
to do the *impractical*.

*Eye has not seen, nor ear heard,
Nor have entered into the heart of man
The things which God has prepared
for those who love Him.*
(1 Corinthians 2:9)

References

(1) J.E Sturdivant, *No Longer Crippled...From Trauma To Triumph*. El Cajon, CA: Christian Services Network, Inc., 2005.

(2) J.E Bamidele Sturdivant, *A Divine Hunger: A Daily Devotional Guide*. Chicago, IL: Godkulture Publishing, 2011.

(3) J.E Bamidele Sturdivant, *Learning to Soar: Life Lessons for Those Facing Life's Challenges*. Chicago, IL: Godkulture Publishing, 2011.

(4) J.E Bamidele Sturdivant, *Daily Confessions for Impacting Your World*. Chicago, IL: Godkulture Publishing, 2012.

(5) J.E Bamidele Sturdivant, *Hearing & Knowing the Voice of God*. Chicago, IL: GodKulture Publishing, 2013.

A New Life

Experiencing lasting healing, demands that you begin a productive relationship with God. You must surrender your life to the Lordship of Jesus Christ. If you have not accepted Jesus Christ as your Lord and Savior, I encourage you to pray the following prayer aloud in order to receive your salvation:

Heavenly Father, I come to you as a sinner through Your Son, Jesus Christ who died and rose on the third day and is now seated at Your right hand. I confess all my sins and I invite Jesus into my life as my Lord and Savior. Thank You Jesus, that my sins are forgiven. Holy Spirit, I invite you to partner with me in my walk with Jesus. In Jesus' Mighty Name, Amen!

This is the wisest decision you have ever made. Please, do not look back! Find a Bible-believing church where the unadulterated Word of God is being preached and begin to worship there regularly. Buy a Bible and study it daily.

Always ask the Holy Spirit to teach you His Word before you study. Welcome to the Kingdom of Light. May the Lord God bless and uphold you In Jesus' Mighty Name, Amen! I am waiting to hear from you. You can contact me through my address towards the end of this book, or by way of my website.

About The Author

J.E Bamidele Sturdivant, Sr. is the pastor of Faith United Ministries and is known worldwide as a blessing to the body of Christ. His unique style of simply, yet powerfully conveying Biblical principles has drawn millions to the cross and set the stage for massive deliverances and healings in the lives of God's people.

A native Washingtonian, J.E Sturdivant has made a divine connection to Nigeria through his God-appointed relationship with his Father in the Lord, E.A Adeboye. Heralded by Newsweek as one of the 50 Most Powerful world leaders, Adeboye has fully received J.E Sturdivant as a special son and poured mightily into his life in immeasurable ways. Adeboye, with the care of a father, named J.E Sturdivant "Bamidele," which is translated to mean *follow me home.*

Their relationship mirrors that of the prophet Elijah and his protégé, Elisha. As with these Biblical men of God, Bamidele has seen the ascension of Adeboye to greater heights in the Lord. In turn, the same mantle has fallen on him. Since their divine connection, Bamidele's ministry has been marked by the miraculous. Countless testimonies of actual resurrections from the dead, healing from cancer and astounding breakthroughs on every level speak to the authenticity of God's hand on his life and ministry.

A master teacher, Bamidele diligently studies to show himself worthy unto God and in the process earned degrees in Ministry. In turn, the sound Biblical truths he shares undoubtedly remind the world that holiness and excellence are the true hallmark of every Christ-follower.

An accomplished author, Bamidele has written *No Longer Crippled...From Trauma To Triumph!*, which outlines the blueprint for a wholistically, successful life. He also authored sections of *From One Brother To Another*, an inspirational devotional for men of all ethnicities, ages, and social backgrounds.

His most recent releases, *A Divine Hunger*, is a forty day devotional guide which challenges every believer to live a life of holiness supported by an appetite for the Master's Presence. *Learning To Soar* is a step-by-step manual that goes to the root of one's adversities and teaches them how to rise above them victoriously. While *Daily Confessions For Impacting Your World*, is a forty day confession tool which outlines that meditating on the truth of God's Word and speaking it, works together with our faith to bring victory every time. Lately, *Hearing and Knowing the Voice of God*, a tool that will equip you to discern His voice, align your life with His Word and deepen your communion with Him.

He was selected as the Guest Chaplain to offer prayer in the United States Senate in the presence of

President Barack Obama, who was serving as United States Senator from Illinois at the time. His anointed and dynamic preaching style has also garnered the attention of other political officials.

He is a greatly esteemed and sought after teacher and evangelist who frequently ministers extensively throughout North America, the Caribbean, Africa, Asia, and Europe. J.E. Bamidele and his wife, Pamela D. "Modupe" have been married for over 37 years, and are the proud parents of four adult children.

Contact Information

For more information, feel free to contact J.E Bamidele Sturdivant using the mediums listed below. Although he cannot respond personally to all correspondences he would love to get your feedback.

J.E.S. Ministries
7905 Fernham Lane
District Heights
Maryland 20747
USA

Phone: 301-736-2383
Website: www.jesturdivantministries.org

Twitter: twitter.com/jesturdivant
Facebook: facebook.com/james.e.sturdivant

You can order additional copies of this book @

www.daforge.com
www.amazon.com
www.barnesandnoble.com